SPIRITUAL
GANGSTA

THE ACCOMPLICES HAVE BEEN
ASSEMBLED. WHAT YOU DO
NEXT IS UP TO YOU!

EMME RAIN

Lanico Media House
LOUISIANA ○ TEXAS ○ ARKANSAS

ISBN: 978-0-9986520-9-2

First Printing 2018, Printed in the United States.

For the apprentices. You guys give me life. We are inspiring one another and showing the world a new kind of hope, one that is tangible. We are showing them that they are not alone as they reach for the higher places they have always felt but could never prove was there... at least until now!

ACKNOWLEDG(E)MENTS

I must acknowledge the subconscious surgeon himself, Adrian Taffinder. You are definitely UK's finest. You held me accountable to ascend rather than become complacent. You taught me to reach deeper into myself. For that, I'm forever grateful.

Montario Hampton, you are one of my best accomplishments. Thank you for being a great business partner and loving son. You made my finishing this book possible by sacrificing sleep to run the store as I stole away to write.

i

INTRODUCTION

No one could have told me years ago that I'd be living this life, doing what I do and teaching the art of ritual. Like many, I felt that it was taboo and had never intentionally included ritual in my life. Oh sure, I had daily, weekly, monthly routines. I had habits. But that's not the same as ritual is it? Is it? Sure, it is!

When I began practicing independent spirituality, I was truly a novice. I had no clue where to begin. And like many, I started with Google, then YouTube. And before long, a new passion was born. I remember pouring hours into researching everything from universal laws to conspiracy theories. (Hey, sometimes those are quite entertaining, thought-provoking, and more often than not, ridiculous. And some are not theories. They are facts. But I digress.)

I put a ton of time into researching rituals. I was, like

many of you reading this book, afraid of making a horrible mistake and ending the world as I know it. I was anxious to put my new knowledge to work and so I began doing basic candle magick, quietly of course. At first, it wasn't any fantastic, quick miracles knocking down my door. But for some reason, ritual was soothing to my soul and so I stayed consistent with it. But then the sparks turned into raging infernos.

I'll never forget the day one of my petitions came barging into my life within moments of lighting the candle charged with my desire. I was blown away! And I was deeply hooked. I had to know if it was a coincidence or if I had happened upon a super power. Had I really just bent my reality with a damn candle? Hell yeah! It was real! But I wasn't fully convinced so I began this scientific experiment with candle magick. My petitions became more varied and even my version of impossible. But time and time again, I was getting what I wanted. And I was becoming who I was supposed to be all along. A spiritual bad ass and master manifestor!

After perfecting it in my own life, I began helping others get what they want to. After all, what fun is there in being the only one who is getting what they want? And after a couple of years of helping others, my good friend, editor and think tank, Jesse Kimmel-Freeman suggested that I do a book to teach more in-depth what I was doing to get the radical results I was getting, not just for myself but for others. This is the why behind this book, and believe me, there is not an untruth in it. When you get real results for as many people as I serve on a daily basis, you have no need to stretch the truth or sell the idea of manifesting.

This book is written to be both entertaining and also empowering. It is easy to understand, to use, and is designed to help you quickly find again necessary information in a crunch. Please note that some of what you read in this book may sound contrary to what you've Googled or watched on a video. I used only my own experience to create this book because that is all I can say has truly worked for me. By no means is this book meant to limit you, however. Intuition is the first part of spirituality. You must get comfortable listening within yourself and following that small voice. There are no hard, fast rules included though I use the word "rule" instead of doing traditional chapter breaks. Nevertheless, these are suggestions, tips, tricks. Feel free to tweak it and make it your own. After all, magick is not truly powerful until it is your own and ritual works best when each piece of it is infused with your own beautiful energy and intention. Happy reading!

RULE NUMBER 1 - KNOW THE NAME OF THE GAME

Ritual. Magick. Energy manipulation. Work. Practice. Roots. Spells. Conjure. The list of terminology on this side is like learning a whole new language. I learn something new every day. The language can get confusing and cause newbies to be lost in the sauce, unsure of what any of it means or how to get it cracking in their lives. For the sake of this book, we're discussing ritual. After all, you cannot spell spiritual without ritual.

Ritual is the intentional, purpose-filled activity of spirituality. For Buddhist, there is chanting. For Muslims, there is prayer. For Christians, there is church ceremony. Weddings are rituals. The list of what we've been doing forever and never considering as ritual is endless. So, we've all participated in some form of it whether we knew or not. The key is to realize you can do it now and become empowered because of it. You can create new rituals to meet your changing spiritual identity. The possibilities are endless.

RULE NUMBER 2 – CREATE, THE INTENTION INTERVENTION

The process of creation through ritual begins with an intention. There is no getting around it. The things we do without intentions, aimless action, is never as powerful as those backed by a goal, an agenda- intention.

If you've been living the highly reactive life, one in which every action is a reaction to your environment, then intention is the intervention you need. Intention will cause you to rise above the noise and elevate your viewpoint so that your decisions, actions, and energy is pointed toward a definite goal which leads to a happier, more fulfilled and certainly more powerful YOU.

The first part of intention is self-awareness. I've met many people who were out trying to live a life programmed into them by their upbringing. They were trying to compete with their neighbors, trying to make their parents proud, or please their significant others. None of those things are wrong, necessarily. However, those things are often not what is authentic for us. None of us are cheap carbon copies. We are Universal masterpieces, one of a kind superstars. Thus, it is important to spend enough time with self that you can discover that which is beautifully unique about you. When you discover that, you're more likely to be able to set clear goals and intentions that are backed by your heart energy.

Now earlier I mentioned aimless action. Well, on a subconscious level, that is very rare. Sometimes we are definitely unconscious about what is driving our actions. However, something is always steering the ship. It could be your pleasures, your pain, your fears, your past experience, your higher self, your guardian spirits, or a plethora of other things/beings. Again, being very present with yourself is the key to finding out what is generally quietly active just outside of your awareness. Being unaware is never a good place to occupy so the powerful ritualist must be a meditator or someone who has worked out some way to stay in touch with self. Otherwise, your rituals will bring you results that are more in alignment with the quiet paradigm than your spoken desires. Words are powerful but paradigms top them every single time.

Rule Number 3 – Eyes on Target

Distractions are common. In an extremely connected and fast pace world, it is easy to lose focus. But success in ritual and spirituality period will require that you master keeping your focus. It would be easy if nothing beckoned for our attention or if we could get rid of distractions, but that is rarely the case. Usually, we just have to decide to ignore that which is not in alignment with our goals and shove ahead. You likely know by now what you want. But do you know why? The number 1 inside killer of focus is not having a clear understanding of why. Why do you want to heal? Get married? Get a new job? Launch a business? Increase your wealth? Expand your influence? When you know why you're doing it, it will make it easier for you to take the proper steps in life and in your ritual work.

Oftentimes, my students and clients ask me about staying true to intention when it seems not to be working.

There is a tendency to want to change the entire plan when something is moving slowly or seemingly not at all. But the truth is, many times it is not the intention or long-term goal that is the problem. The problem is persevering through the dead time, that is time used to fuel and grow your desire, to juice it up and prep it for life.

Notice, women usually find out they are pregnant a long time before a baby comes out, or even months before there are any physical sign of the new life within them. It is the same in spiritual work. You are birthing a brand-new thing into your life and it takes time to give it enough energy to live. A woman doesn't wait until she is showing, and her labor is in full swing to begin adjusting her lifestyle for the new baby that is coming. Neither should you await proof to keep your work going toward that which you have decided to create via ritual.

Patience is a virtue in this form of work and cannot be overemphasized. It will help you stay focused, help you align your creative actions and not self-sabotage at the first sign of opposition or challenge.

In ritual, the target is your intention. If you have set an intention to become debt-free and boost your credit score by 20 points, then that is your target. You have to keep that keenly in focus as you prepare your ritual. The trick to it is not to go into the ritual thinking about how much you "wish" your credit score was higher and you had no debt. You must go into it thankful that your credit score is higher and that you have no debt. That subtle difference means everything. So you are thinking about how good it feels to have good credit. You are feeling the freedom of not owing money on your home, automobiles, land and credit cards. You are going in as if you have what you seek. You are simply bringing it into the physical realm.

As you prep candles, handle herbs, oils, crystals, water or whatever else you are doing, you are holding this intention clearly, keeping your eyes on the target. Every piece of the ritual is now saturated with your intention and the target is in sight. This makes for POWERFUL energy manipulation.

RULE NUMBER 4 – THE ACCOMPLICES

Now that you're clear about what you seek to create and why, it's time to gather up the tools that will aid and abet you throughout the ritual. These are corresponding items that carry a compatible vibration to what you are building.

When most people think of rituals, they almost immediately think of candles, but ritual has always been a huge part of our lives even without our knowing it. So a bath can become a ritual of cleansing and purification, especially when corresponding herbs like blessed thistle, hyssop or lavender are used. Cleaning your home can become a ritual, especially when you sage and clear energy as you go about it. Feng Shui is popular because it shows you how to keep good energy in your home simply by arranging it a certain way and using various color combinations. All of this is ritual, and all of the items used are accomplices to your end game.

So, let's first talk candles. Candles are an invaluable resource in ritual. They provide an extra energy boost and can be programmed with intention. In fact, anything can be programmed with your intention and all ritual tools should be. But candles are special because the fire is continually lifting that intention as it burns. While there are already a lot of blogs and information on candle colors, let me give you my brief overview of which colors I use and why:

➢ Black – protection, cloaking, dark energy work, power, dominance, blockbuster, various deities, for balance when burned with a white candle to denote yin and yang energy, divination, scrying, primordial restoration/healing, necromancy.

➢ Blue — throat chakra work, business, career, healing, harmony, peace, mental clarity, loyalty, various deities, male baby blessings, Mercury energy rituals, communication work, some matrimonial work (usually paired with red).

➢ Brown — grounding, past life work, some careers and businesses, some ancestral work, necromancy, security, various deities.

➢ Purple — third eye and crown work, spirit evocation and invocation, protection, work with higher self or oversoul, raise vibrations of an atmosphere or ritual, divination, powerful color to add to orange and yellow for creativity.

➢ Red — love, passion, lust, tantra, war, protection, power, courage, momentum, energy, root chakra work, marriage, Mars energy rituals, various deities, powerful enchantment when used with pink, silver and gold.

➢ Pink — love, femininity, friendship, enchantments, heart chakra work (works well paired with green), female baby blessings, fertility (usually paired with green), glamour work, sweetening work, various deities.

➢ Orange — sacral chakra work, creativity, happiness/joy (especially when paired with yellow), fall equinox work (usually paired with brown), self-esteem work, various deities.

➢ Yellow — solar plexus work, cheerfulness, confidence, fresh start, summer solstice work, Sun energy work, self-esteem, various deities, energetic balancing, abundance when paired with green.

➢ Green — heart chakra work, healing, connection to the earth, grounding, money, abundance, prosperity, restorative work, serenity/peace work (pairs well with blue), various deities, fertility work, Spring equinox work.

➢ Silver — feminine energy, receptivity, divine connections, lunar work, connecting with maternal lineage, enchantments, emotional healing and balance.

➢ Gold — masculine energy, empowerment, alignment, divine connections, solar work/sun energy work, connecting with paternal lineage, wealth, riches, luck, dominance, luxury.

Another well-known but often underutilized tool is herbalism. Now, it goes without saying that herbs and natural remedies are making a huge impact on the lives of people around the globe. Nature medicine has never died and likely will not because even without all the governmental studies to prove efficacy, there is a long tradition of treating many ailments with what we can pluck out of the backyard.

However, magickal use of herbs is a different ballgame. It doesn't require as many tests, studies, etc. because for the most part, herbs used in ritual are not ingested. As always, use precautions and learn all you can about any herb you are handling. And if you are creating magickal teas and tinctures, make sure they are safe to put on skin or consume. Now with that MAJOR disclaimer out of the way, let's dig in.

There are more herbs than I have time to write about. I remember in the beginning of my journey, I Googled "herbal magic" and quickly discovered what would become my top 5 go to herbs. However, I look at my herbal cabinet now and swear that I'm a collector of sorts. I cannot go into a metaphysical store without picking up a few additional herbs each time. When I opened my own store, the first items I added to the list of must haves, even before candles, were herbs. So, to say I love them is an understatement. Still, I won't bother you guys with an endless list. So, let's talk Emme Rain's top 12 herbs for ritual use:

1. Angelica Root – hey, everyone is entitled to their favorites and this is for sure my favorite herb and my constant companion. If I could have an herbal familiar, it would be Angelica Root. This herb is a powerhouse. It can be used in healing, feminine power awakening, protection, empowerment, for amplifying any work, enchantments, and a plethora of other rituals. It is THE premier herb for any worker and a delight for use in ancestor and deity veneration.

2. Patchouli — so, I'll be the first to admit, this is one that had to grow on me. I couldn't stomach how strong it was and I didn't find the smell pleasing to be honest. (I know I'm in the minority here.) However, I found myself running back to this superpower over and over. I found myself using it in my money rituals, protection rituals, cleansing rituals. It is great for lust spells and fertility as well. In fact, when I looked up, I was having to replace my patchouli stash more

frequently than my Angelica Root. It really is the one you don't want to ritual without.

3. Lavender — so lavender is not the scent I prefer smelling, but it is indeed an herb that you should not practice without. It's most popular for its uses in sleep pillows and the scent is a regular one in many household products. However, lavender is also protective, calming, healing and clearing. It can be used in home blessings and marriage work. It has strong properties of love and longevity. So, the uses for lavender are expansive. It is the base for many of my oils and body butters and has been a friend to me in my workings.

4. Lemon Verbena — this is definitely my second favorite herb for a thousand reasons. Let me state the obvious one first. THE SMELL IS FANTASTIC! I could shout it from the rooftops. I love lemon and those who purchase my oils can likely attest to that, but the lemon verbena is a nice mild blend of lemony, grassy, crisp goodness that sucks you in. It can be used in enchantments, glamours, amplifying workings, clearing, cleansing, divine feminine rituals, as offerings to the goddesses, and much more. I personally find that lemon verbena is great in ancestral workings dealing with maternal healings. I also use it to break baneful magick. Get some. Get plenty!

5. Lemongrass — why break the chain, right? I love lemongrass. The protective and healing qualities are outstanding. The ease of use is fantastic. This herb is a principle component of many powerful oil blends like Van Van and more. I use it often in balancing and self-mastery rituals, etheric cord cuttings, blessings and bounty rituals, in workings with the 7 African Powers and an endless list of other rituals. When I am clearing karma, removing toxicity and attachments, this herb is my partner.

6. Rue — nothing protects your home and family like rue. Rue is a protective giant. It can be sprinkled around your home and even worn for the properties it holds. I use it in protections, reversals, and even cloaking rituals.

7. Catnip — I do a lot of enticement work and catnip is my go-to. It blends well with other herbs that enchant, call or enhance libido and can even be smoked or consumed as a tea when couples want that extra boost. It can be used in love spells, taming a mate, calling a mate, tantric practices and much more.

8. Allspice — personally, allspice is my third favorite herb. It is great in manifestation, money, prosperity, longevity, and even self-mastery workings. There isn't much you cannot do with allspice and it looks so awesome floating around

in a magickal oil blend, so it is a frequent find in Magickal Mystic oils.

9. Coltsfoot Leaf — money, money, money, money (I hear that in my head like a song every time I walk past my coltsfoot leaf herbs.) But this sleeping giant has a lot of other properties that are often overlooked. It works well in reversing lack paradigms, in speeding up the workings you include it in, for protection of assets and more.

10. Clove — I would not be a spiritual gangsta if it were not for clove. The scent is strong and the properties stronger. I mainly use cloves for protection, enchantments, friendship and amicable workings like peaceful divorces, etc. It can be used for money work and also for business boosts. One of my favorite uses for cloves though is in workings with Ganesha and Lakshmi. Both love the energy and powerful, lasting vibration of cloves.

11. Blue Flag Root — the primary use of this herb is money and wealth. It is great in creating, building and growing a business, starting a new career and attracting random gifts and acts of kindness.

12. Cinnamon — Protective? Check. Enticing? Check. Intense? Check. Loving? Check. There is not much cinnamon cannot do. It is one of those herbs that can stand on its own. From protection to prosperity work, it works. It can enhance any

ritual or working and increase the speed in which a manifestation comes through. It is known to attract love, money, new people and yet protect against baneful energies.

I would love to go on and on. It was very difficult to narrow the list down to only 12. At original writing of this book, I had 30 on the list. But again, the purpose of this book is not herbalism. However, I would like to at least list a few honorable mentions that should be purchased and used frequently: dill seed, blessed thistle, Althea root, mugwort, calendula, roses, coriander seed, rosemary, watercress, eucalyptus, anise star or seed, mandrake, chicory, and licorice.

Some of you have done Magickal Mystic rituals with me. I built my brand from powerful oils that became a HUGE part of the life-changing rituals you all have witnessed. So, I want to list a few of those oils and what you can use that may likely already be around your home.

➢ Manifestation Blend – used to enhance your manifestation work. It adds energy and clarity.
➢ Impenetrable Defense – used to seal your aura and keep you protected from negative energy.
➢ Meditation Blend – used to calm the mind and encourage the brain to sync into theta waves for relaxation.
➢ Healing Arts – used to energize and align the energetic body. This oil is blended with herbs and oils

that encourage both physical and spiritual healing and has been reported to alleviate pain when used in conjunction with meditation.

➢ Lasting Love – used to give and call for the vibration of long-term commitment.

➢ Generational Wealth – used to call forward unclaimed knowledge, opportunities and wealth throughout the bloodline and bring it into physical manifestation.

➢ Cease and Desist – used to stop any magickal attacks, hexes, binds, curses or runs of bad luck.

None of the Magickal Mystic oils are FDA approved and should not be consumed, of course. These are curios sold for magickal potency and ritual use only. The power is in the intention and energy infused into them. By that same token, you likely already have oils that could be infused with extra intention and used in ritual, such as: olive oil (I prefer extra virgin), safflower oil, walnut oil, rosemary, lavender, lemon, eucalyptus, cinnamon, frankincense essential oils. Whatever you have can become magickal when powered by your energy and your determination to create with it. Never feel that your ritual cannot be effective until you're using all the props and tools long time ritualists are using. We all must start somewhere. And I will tell you this, your toolkit will grow with time and practice. Crystals and stones will be added and adored for their many properties. Other pieces that are significant only to you. THAT is what is going to fuel your rituals and make them work for you.

RULE NUMBER 5 – THE BIG GUNS

Ritual is much more than candles, herbs and oils. Ritual is a blending of all things that are in agreement with your intention and putting them together in a way that is conducive to the end you seek. If it were as simple as having all the stuff on the list, more people would practice ritual. But there is more to the picture. This is where the big guns come out.

One of the least used aspects of ritual for spiritual development and ascension is sacred geometry, or geometric pattern period, whether you find it sacred or not. For some, this may seem complicated. People indeed do often overcomplicate anything math related, and geometry is no exception. Still, understanding basic shapes and symbols will aid you in creating rituals that work.

Below are some basics on shapes and symbols and

how I use them. This is not an exhaustive list but definitely should be used as a quick reference guide. Remember to use your intuition and trust it. Some of what is listed below came to me through study, but most of it came intuitively. I have not yet regretted defining and redefining my spiritual practice through my intuition.

- ❖ Circle – the almighty circle, a symbol that represents wholeness, completion, eternity, oneness, and even protection and separation.
- ❖ Square — symbol of grounding, stability, solidarity, unification, agreement, and a primary symbol in elemental magick.
- ❖ Triangle/Pyramid — first let me say that these are not really the same and that confuses people many times during practice because any single face of the pyramid is a triangle except the base which is a square. The triangular shape is all about channeling power, going out and coming in. It represents movement of intention, information, energy. It also represents focus and clarity. The pyramid has a solid base which adds the ability to store power, information, energy. That solid base also represents the grounding of that which is channeled.
- ❖ Star — symbol of Spirit in many traditions, and also elemental magick when Spirit or ether is considered the 5th element, but it so much more. The star carries the energy of many triangles with the benefit of a

center which can contain power, information, energy. The more points, the more potential for dispersion of energy to various intended goals.

❖ Pentacle — because this is the symbol of the 5-point star enclosed in a circle, I decided to separate it for the sake of understanding various uses. Known as a premier protective symbol, many people still don't know why. The star can represent multi-directional movement of energy. The circle around it represents wholeness and protection. It is the picture of activity that allows you to operate without exposing yourself. It protects your energetic field while allowing you to still move things in and out at will. It also brings a singular focus to your multi-directional movements.

❖ Metatron's Cube — the cube of creation is probably the least understood and most often over complicated geometric figure. I won't get into a lesson other than to say that this cube does indeed hold the key to creation because it represents the birthing of light itself. The center is the place of conception and through motion, all that is first conceived in the middle is shifted through the various pieces until it is made entire enough to become an independent entity of its own. That is really an over-simplification, but this is the most important piece as it pertains to ritual and also to mentalism.

As you can see, just working with these shapes and

patterns, you can revolutionize your ritual in no time flat. Other powerhouse patterns to understand work with are: spiral, tree of life, flower of life, seed of life.

Another aspect of ritual that is a really big gun is incantation. An incantation is, more simply put, a prayer. It is a statement of intention, gratitude, or a set of words infused with special power. Many people fail to speak to their rituals. They do not understand the value of words, whether words of plain understanding or words from beyond this realm. Mystical uttering has always been around. Even in biblical times, there was often a reference made to moaning or wailing women. Battlecries were popular during hand-to-hand combat. Why? Because sounds have their own vibration and the right combination of sound can invoke a presence and even open a portal to get you the desired effect.

If you have never studied sounds and the effect it has on your brain and body, on water, on everything around us, then you want to make that a priority. Sound has even been used to move heavy objects from place to place. It is a force all its own. And in ritual, it is your heavy hitter. The spiritual world responds to vibration, every realm having its own. When you sound like what you desire, you will possess it.

RULE NUMBER 6 – STRIKE FORCE

After the whole gang is together, you are ready to make a move. I call this the strike force because these are your hitters, your group of mystic bandits who are helping you to ascend through the noise of this realm into your power, whatever that ends up looking like for you.

A word here I want to interject- not everyone practices ritual for the same reason. Thus, trying to lay out a how to on rituals is tough because our rituals should be as authentic as our fingerprints. I do much of my work via social media and I see a lot of people who copy their mentors or those who seem to be getting the results they want. After awhile, a lot of people give up because they believe that it doesn't work for them since their own results are not as stellar. The issue is not ritual. The issue is personalization. To bring this point home, 5 men could have dated the same woman and had very different results because each man is different thus eliciting a different response from her. It's not just about the squad, but also how you utilize them.

In watching sports, I've seen people trade various players just to have those players go somewhere else and be phenomenal. The synergy of some players is not as strong as it is with others. The atmosphere makes a difference. The coach damn sure makes a huge difference. Ultimately, my point is that a candle in my hand and a candle in yours are not going to be nor should it be the same. Even when you have 10 people working toward physical healing, the energy and intention going into the setup of ritual should be very individual. This is what has led to me having such an overwhelming success in my ritual outcomes and why people continue to flock to me for personalized rituals beyond the group rituals I do weekly.

Now let's discuss YOUR strike force. Not every player may get equal play, and that's absolutely okay. For some, the candle, the circle and the square are home for you. That's where you feel powerful and if so, then make those your hitters and build a strong relationship there. For others, you're going to be all purpose. You'll be using everything at various times and sometimes at the same time. Trust me, I've had to put together some extremely large rituals with all sorts of happenings going on in it. The biggest deal is to put in the personal time necessary to know your team and which part is the best element to add to whatever you are working on.

As you set up your ritual space, you must remember always that you need a blank slate to begin with. You don't want stagnation to exist where you are making magick happen. So, cleansing your area is necessary before assembling your team. Personally, I use Spirit Knows Best room mists to get the job done quickly and prepare the atmosphere for what may go down. Saging is fantastic but not always necessary. Sage is a strong clearing agent. If you have a dedicated space, you may have built up some sweetness and love there too. Sage wipes everything. Sometimes, sweet grass or Palo Santo can be just as protective without being harsh to the workings you've already done to consecrate the space.

After your space is ready, it is time to begin putting the pieces where they go. Arrange your candles, herbs, stones, consecrated pieces, figurines where they are most beneficial according to how sacred geometry would call for as it pertains to your intention. For instance, if you are doing a ritual of protection from all things negative, you may put a single candle in the middle of a circle to represent you. You may surround that candle with protective herbs, stones and figurines. Or if you were doing a money ritual to break poverty and bring wealth, you may use 2 or 3 candles to destroy past paradigms, create a new wealth reality, and carry it into the future. Again, it is really all about what various things mean to you. That is where the power truly resides. Here is where your intuition will rule supreme. Listen to what feels right. Do not be afraid to make adjustments until you feel comfortable. After all, you are commanding some powerful players. You don't want to send them off to battle haphazardly. You want to have given care and consideration to what and who and when. STRIKE FORCE, GO!

RULE NUMBER 7 – GETTING RID OF THE EVIDENCE

"What do I do with the material when I finish?"

I am pretty sure I get that question at least twice a day. Proper discard of magickal items is important and often over complicated as well. The biggest issue is not to hold on to stagnant energy or anything that absorbed it and not to release anything with your energy attached to it.

Candles are a big part of ritual. I often use 7-14-day glass jar candles, also called novena or vigil candles. These particular ones need to be properly discarded since the glass is left behind after the ritual. If I used blood, hair or any personal effects in ritual, I wash or boil the jar until it is clear of any of my energy. Another method I've used, depending upon what kind of ritual I am doing is break the glass that once held the candle and bury it. They can also be thrown in a river, not a lake, though I do not advocate littering.

As it pertains to your crystals, normally you can clear and reuse but not always. If you do heavy healing work and use stones to transmute energy, to absorb sickness, disease, and poverty, then you don't want to reuse them very often because they are taking on that energy. Thus, when a stone is full of what you want to be rid of, it is better to take it away from the property and bury it again.

Generally, statues can be kept and cleared with a brisk rub down with a warm damp washcloth but can also be cleared with sage. There may be times when you have to discontinue use and, in that moment,, you want to release the energy you have stored in the statue and then throw it away. Some give their ritual statue pieces away, but I really do not recommend that and I do not accept anyone else's previously used statues. I had a friend to give me a piece and it was later revealed that it had been tampered with energetically and it was a disruption to my life rather than a help.

There are many ways to handle discarding magickal items, but this is the general rule of thumb I follow in my own practice:

- None of your blood, hair, nails or personal effects thrown away. Wash or burn them before discarding.
- Protection and hexing items that absorbed negativity or sent negativity should be discarded away from your

home and any property you own. Many of these items can be buried at an offsite location if you want it to keep working after the ritual has ended.

- Break candle glasses that were representative of that you wish to be removed from your life and throw them away.

- Offerings that were a part of the ritual can be given to nature. Usually I leave at the foot of a tree. You can use any wine, water or juice to give a final gratitude offering to the energies who assisted you as you pour it out.

- Ashes from burnings may be kept, especially in wealth work or can be scattered in the wind. It depends upon how you feel about it. If you keep your ashes in a jar, you must decide upon how long you will continue and what will be the final use for them. Personally, I find ashes to be the perfect offering to wind/air energies.

RULE NUMBER 8 – THE AFTERMATH

The physical ritual is only one part of the work you do. What happens when the candles burn out and the remains are discarded is just as important as putting the pieces of the ritual together.

There are two schools of thought and I'm going to explain how both are relevant and it requires discernment to know which one is most needed in any given situation.

The first school of thought is to do it and forget about it. This isn't one I practice often, but there are times when it is absolutely necessary to release your attachment to the ritual and the outcome. Sometimes, the worst thing you can do is keep obsessing about whatever problem you just addressed through your work. In fact, worry is always counter-productive. Anxious thought is an enemy to the good energy you just sent to your desired manifestation. Obsessing about how it will happen is worrying. Truth be told, you never need to worry about how or if you'll miss it. You're more likely to miss open doors when you're afraid you will than you are when you choose to trust the guiding light of the Universe.

Now on the other hand, if you're building something major, the ritual is a great place to push a huge amount of energy into what you're building. But that does not have to be the only energy your desire gets. It is perfectly acceptable to schedule time to feed more energy into what you just did ritual for, and in fact, I often encourage it. The key is not to do it in worry, fear, doubt or desperation.

After I put together my ritual, I spend some time charging it up with my intentions before lighting up. Then, during the hours or days it is burning, I come through and add more good, clean energy to it, often using statements of gratitude to fuel it along. After it burns out, I am in a state of pure delight while I dismantle it. If it is going to possibly be a complex creation, I will leave the petition on my altar and continue burning smaller candles over it for a period of time, usually until the full moon when my petitions are burned. Even if I burn the petition right away, I still choose to wake up each morning in a state of gratitude concerning it. I speak words to remind me to stay open and loose, like "I am so happy that I have what I desire or better in a way that is in alignment with my highest purposes and for my highest good."

Now let me say this, there are times when you'll do ritual and you will feel yourself completely release the situation, petition or desire. It will be as if it never happened. This is usually when I receive the swiftest answer when even without me choosing to forget about it, it is forgotten anyway. Do not be alarmed. Sometimes, your higher-self steps in and does you a solid without you even realizing it.

A plethora of emotions may hit you before, during and after ritual. It can especially be a wild ride after ritual though. Anxiety may try to crop up from time to time. We feel what we feel. You don't have to fight it or deny it. Just do not attach to any emotion other than joy. Let them pass through you. Don't give any contrary emotion any additional energy by interacting with it. Simply witness it and keep going. You'll be amazed at how quickly they pass when there is no energy within you for them.

Sometimes, right after ritual, your actual situation may appear to get worse. Disintegration is rarely a bad sign. Any movement, no matter how your logical mind judges it, is most probably a good thing. I did a ritual for a lady who wanted to bring her marriage closer together. A few days after the ritual completed, her husband came home and packed his bags. Needless to say, she was VERY upset and disheartened. She messaged me daily asking what else she could do. But the answer that continued to come was nothing. She needed to wait. After 3 weeks, she asked for a full refund. I told her that

I would refund her but that when she got what she paid me for, she'd owe me double the fee for the inconvenience. 2 months later, she inboxed for my PayPal information again and sent double and a huge tip.

Part of her getting what she wanted was her losing what was in the place of it. He left her thinking that he no longer loved her. She ended up going through a minor illness. When he heard about it, he came running to her. This opened up a dialogue in which she became aware of some stuff she'd previously been clueless about. They were able to restore the bond and make it stronger. When he moved back in, in her words, "the version of him that came back was worth the pain of him leaving."

So, you see, it is important to detach from the how and when. You don't know just what it will cost on the physical plane for you to have what you desire. You need a great deal of trust that divine order will bring you exactly what is most needed, which could also be something totally different than what you asked for.

I had one client who came to me for a raise at her job. Truth is, however, what she needed was more income. So, while the work was still going, she got fired. She overslept one morning. I encouraged her to stay as positive as possible. On her way to her mom's house one morning, she heard about a business that was hiring. She said that when she went down to apply for the job, there was a long line of people seeking the same job. Just so happen, however, that she ran into an old friend. While chatting, they started talking about the jewelry my client used to make and how she would love to purchase a particular kind of necklace if she'd ever make it. Long story short, she didn't get the job, but that day led her to pulling out her jewelry kit to make a single necklace for an old friend. Now she has a $5000 per month work from home business making jewelry... by appointment only. That was almost twice her income at her job.

Again, ritual does not guarantee quick results. In fact, I encourage my students to keep your work working. Ritual does not always bring happy circumstances. Sometimes, it is through pain that you receive your request. Just like pregnancy and labor, it can be uncomfortable. But the end result is most certainly worth it. If what you desire is not worth a couple of tears, then it probably does not even warrant rituals in the first place.

When you put a ritual together for a specific desire, you lose a lot of physical control over how things will flow from there. However, it doesn't matter much how it flows because if you have done your job well, it will most definitely be what is best for you on all levels and dimensions.

EPILOGUE

I've been faithfully and intentionally practicing ritual for years. Of course, we've all been practicing ritual unaware all of our lives. Because of bath rituals, the people of the world generally smell pretty good. Because of house cleaning rituals, most houses we visit are relatively clean. Because of sexual rituals, the world is thoroughly populated. If you see all repetitive action as a form of ritual, it helps you stop judging the word. Ritual is not evil, witchcraft, or even mystical. It doesn't become that until you intend it to be.

Not to get on a soapbox, but it is so important that we redefine our lives for ourselves. We should never borrow someone else's limitations, definitions, offenses or judgments. While it feels safer to do so, it can be oppressive and painful. Indeed, there is no greater pain than the pain of living beneath our potential and without our hearts' desires.

It is my sincerest hope that everyone who reads this book is enlightened, encouraged and empowered. Do not be afraid to use the power around you and definitely that which is inherent. You deserve a better life because you desire one. You deserve to build it according to your own specifications. Ritual is a tool to help you do just that. With that being said, welcome to the family, creators. We've been waiting on you!

SPELLS AND RITUALS

SELF-HEALING RITUAL

Items Needed:

- ❖ 1 Novena or taper candle, white or pink
- ❖ Rosemary essential oil
- ❖ Green glitter
- ❖ Bowl of water
- ❖ Clear quartz
- ❖ Rose quartz
- ❖ Unakite crystals

Dress the candle with 3 drops of rosemary oil to represent healing of your past, present and future self. Rub the oil into or onto the candle. Add sprinkles of green glitter to represent nurturing and abundant energy.

Put the bowl of water right behind the candle. Drop two drops of Rosemary oil in the water. Surround both with the crystals. Take a moment to set your intentions for healing virtues to flow through your soul and through your DNA. See your body, spirit and energy all being repaired and hold that visualization for about a minute. Then light your candle in a state of happy gratitude.

SELF-MASTERY SPELL

Items Needed:

❖ Red jar candle

❖ Black thread or string

❖ Sea salt

❖ Circular mirror to go under the candle

Dress your candle with your self-mastery oil. See it as if it is a representation of you. Imagine yourself full of power and energy. Then, tie the black string around the glass to represent controlling that power and energy. Put a circle of sea salt all around the candle on the mirror if possible but around it if not. This is for protection because you want to be in control of yourself.

You say a brief incantation:

> *I am energy. It flows all through me. I stand confidently at the helm. I am mastery.*

Light it and give thanks to the Universe for fortifying your mind and helping you attain your goal.

BREAK ALL ATTACHMENTS SPELL

Items Needed:

- ❖ Black candle
- ❖ 4 Pieces of bloodroot
- ❖ 4 Pieces of black onyx
- ❖ 4 Pieces of smoky quartz
- ❖ Rue
- ❖ Hyssop
- ❖ High John Root
- ❖ 4 glasses or bowls of water with drops of eucalyptus and cinnamon oil

Dress candle with the Cease and Desist or Impenetrable Defense oil. If you have neither, use the cinnamon essential oil.

Put the rue, hyssop and high john root shavings into your mortar and use pestle to grind together. For extra umph, add mugwort, astragalus root, or Angelica root. After blended thoroughly, sprinkle in an unbroken counterclockwise circle around the candle you are burning.

Place the 4 bowls/glasses of water at the south, west, north and east position around the candle. In between the bowls of water, put pieces of smoky quartz. Place the black onyx closer inside the circle around the candle itself. This onyx is to absorb the energy others are shooting at you or to deflect those who are trying to drain you.

The last part is the bloodroot. Place them around the candle as well, right outside of the onyx but closer than the bowls of water and smoky quartz.

The whole time, you are seeing yourself break free from all the ropes and chains that may be attached and affecting you. You want to visualize you rising to high that the cords snap and break, even. Then you want to see fire consume all that was attached. You want to see your magick and power as undeniable and that you are getting what you want.

If you have wrestled with low energy because of being drained by others, call back your energy, and see yourself absorbing it back through the filters and cleaners of the smoky quartz.

SHUT THE FUCK UP SPELL

Items Needed:

- ❖ Person's name on brown paper bag
- ❖ A dab of super glue
- ❖ Freezer bag
- ❖ Animal tongue purchased from the grocery store (a red pepper can be substituted here)
- ❖ Vinegar
- ❖ Juice of a lemon
- ❖ Alum

In your cauldron, mix the vinegar, lemon and pepper. If you can find some black mustard seed, throw that in to bring more confusion and chaos to them.

Take the tongue. Speak clearly your intentions but keep it simple. Stab through the tongue with your ritual knife with some aggression. Place it in the cauldron mixture and soak it thoroughly while imagining what you intend. Take the tongue back out and over the slit you made when you stabbed it, put the paper with their name with a dab of super glue. Imagine that you are permanently ridded of their harsh words. Now, pour the cauldron mixture into your freezer bag and place the tongue inside with the name glued on. Try to get it as airtight as possible, roll and seal it and then cover in aluminum foil with the shiny side inward. Place in the back of your freezer where it will not be disturbed. Or you can take it and bury it by your favorite tree so that a guardian is watching over it.

SELF-HEALING USING OBATALA

Items Needed:

- ❖ White vigil candle
- ❖ Lavender oil or herb
- ❖ Lemongrass
- ❖ Angelica root
- ❖ Rosemary
- ❖ Marigold
- ❖ Peppermint oil or herb

Poke 3 holes in the candle clockwise. Put a piece of your hair or nail clipping in the holes. Add oils and herbs. Rub your hands together vigorously for about 45 secs. Place hands around the candle and close your eyes. Infusion your intent to heal into the candle. Imagine pushing every problem into it to be transmuted.

Say an oration to Obatala and then light your candle. Be sure to make an offering to him as well. To enhance the power, you can surround your candle with clear quartz and obsidian, even citrine. Unakite is another great healing stone. You can also use the Magickal Mystic Obatala oil if you have it in place of the other oils.

HEALING RITUAL FOR THE BODY

Items Needed:

- ❖ Epsom or sea salt
- ❖ Eucalyptus (oil or herb)
- ❖ Lemon essential oil
- ❖ Peppermint (oil or herb)
- ❖ Blue candle

Dress the candle in the essential oils or place herbs in or around the candle. Other great herbs to use are blessed thistle and motherwort.

Run a really warm bath with the salts and essential oils and herbs in the water. Light 7 tea lights in the bathroom and as you light each, call in the energies of your healers, the healing ancestors, angels and whatever other energies you use for healing.

Place the blue candle in the middle of the white tea lights and declare softly but with confidence:

> *I am restored.*
> *Energy renewed.*
> *Body rejuvenated.*

Light the blue candle.

Get in the tub. Make it your intention to wash away stagnant energy, dis-ease and dys-function. Keep softly or mentally repeating the affirmation as you sit down in the water.

Imagine the water absorbing all the illness, negativity and stagnant energy from your body.

EMOTIONAL BALANCE RESTORATION

Items Needed:

- ❖ Blue and white chime or votive candles
- ❖ Rosemary (herb)
- ❖ Angelica root (herb)
- ❖ Lavender (herb)
- ❖ Shatavari root (herb)
- ❖ Chamomile (herb)
- ❖ Equilibrium, Harmonize, or lavender essential oils
- ❖ Mirror
- ❖ Fresh roses
- ❖ Glass of red wine

Dress the candles with your oils with a clear intention to heal and balance your emotions. See those candles as representations of you, your physical and spiritual self. Place the candles on the mirror. Then surround the candles in the infinity symbol, a sideways figure eight, with herbs. Place the fresh roses and the glass of wine behind the ritual but not on the mirror. Imagine being in your own private oasis and absorbing beautiful energy. I recommend doing this ritual at least once a month though I generally do it 3 or 4 times a month.

MAGICKAL MONEY MAGNET

Items Needed:

- ❖ Green or gold 7 day candle
- ❖ Coltsfoot (herb)
- ❖ Dill seed (herb)
- ❖ Blue flag root (herb)
- ❖ Allspice (herb)
- ❖ Fast Money essential oil
- ❖ Manifestation essential oil
- ❖ Generational Wealth essential oil
- ❖ Chamomile essential oil
- ❖ Cedarwood essential oil
- ❖ Green aventurine
- ❖ Citrine
- ❖ Pyrite
- ❖ Carnelian
- ❖ Clear quartz
- ❖ Live plant or flowers
- ❖ Petition with money desired and/or items you seek to buy

Dress your candles with herbs and oils. Put a string of your hair in the candle. Surround it with your crystals. Place a glass of water or wine on one side of the ritual. Place your live plant or flowers on the other side. Make sure the petition is under the candle.

Sit with your candle and imagine that you and the candle are one. See it bringing the items you desire, the money you desire. Keep your hands on the candle until you feel the tingles between your palms. Then light it and say an oration to your ancestors. Stay in space of gratitude. I recommend this ritual be done on a Thursday.

ABOUT THE AUTHOR

Emme Rain, the alter ego of Lacresha Hayes, is the world renowned intuitive who has been making a lot of waves with her mysticism and spiritual work. As a leader and mentor to thousands, she has helped several closet psychics, mediums and readers to come forward and find success.

Emme/Lacresha is the owner of Magickal Mystic, LLC and the proprietor of Elle's Cafe, the magickal apprenticeship offered to select individuals. With over 600 rituals and thousands of spells under her belt, she has tens of thousands of testimonials concerning her work.

Emme's primary focus is manifestation and understanding the universal laws and how they all work together. She teaches an actionable version of the law of attraction and brings powerful revelation to those who listen about what is missing to create what they desire. Currently, Emme lives in Louisiana but travels all over the country with her Manifest Your Destiny Tour.

Remember this
It is YOUR destiny
so manifest the hell out of it!

Emma Rain

Made in the USA
Las Vegas, NV
22 April 2023